Another C

THE ADVENTURES

Simon & Barklee in England

By David J. Scherer

Illustrations by Kara Richardson

A publication of ExplorerMedia
ISBN: 0-9704661-1-0

To order additional copies, books, or other educational materials, call or visit our website:
www.simonandbarklee.com

Cataloging-in-Publication Data:

Scherer, David J.
Simon & Barklee in England / by David J. Scherer; illustrations by Kara Richardson. --1st ed. p. cm. -- (Another country calling, the adventures of Simon & Barklee.)
ISBN: 0-9704661-1-0
SUMMARY: American travelers Simon & Barklee visit England, where their adventures and travels introduce them to the history, culture and traditions of a fascinating country.

1. England--Description and travel--juvenile litrature.2. Great Britain--History--Juvenile literature. 3 Great Britain--Social life and customs--Juvenile literature. I. Title.

942
DA632.S34 2001 QBI01-200066

Illustrations by Kara Richardson
Printed in Singapore by Star Standard Industries (S) Pte Ltd

Simon & Barklee in England

Once, there were two unlikely world travelers. One was Simon T. McTwill, a golden canary with a beautiful voice. The other was Barklee, a frisky terrier with a brave heart. The canary wanted to sing in famous cities around the world, the dog dreamed of adventure. They were the best of friends, and they knew there was no better way to learn about the world and its people than to experience them. So that's what they did ... they set out to see the world.

For my brothers
Don, Mike and Wally.

Table of Contents

Simon &
Barklee in
England

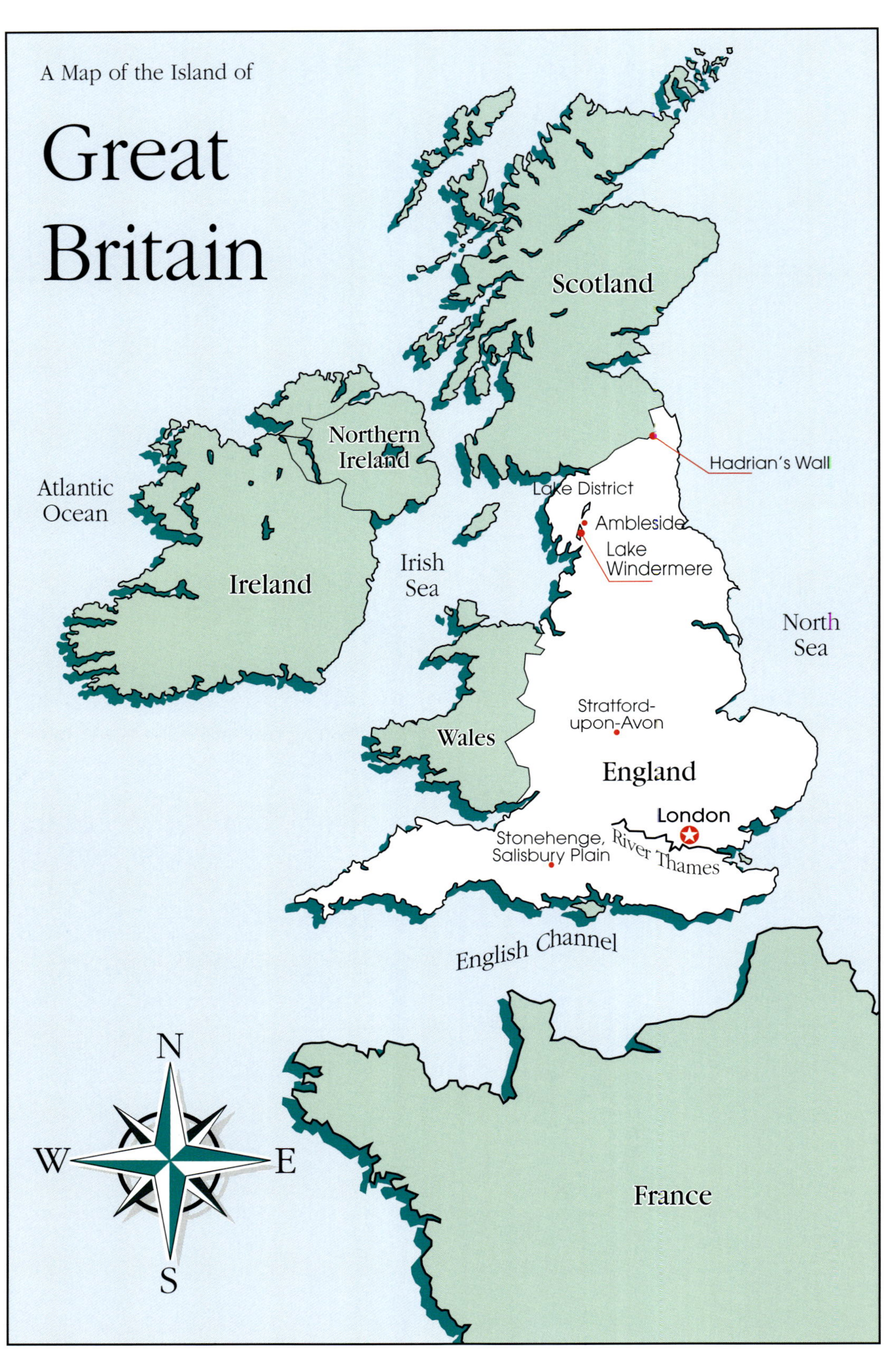
A Map of the Island of
Great Britain
Scotland
Northern Ireland
Atlantic Ocean
Ireland
Hadrian's Wall
Lake District
Ambleside
Lake Windermere
Irish Sea
North Sea
Wales
Stratford-upon-Avon
England
London
Stonehenge, Salisbury Plain
River Thames
English Channel
France
N
W
E
S

The Adventure Begins

Simon and Barklee felt the first tingle of excitement as their airplane came close to London, England. Simon smoothed his feathers and tightened his seat belt. His stomach gurgled with nervousness. He had been invited to sing at the world-famous ***Royal Albert Hall***. Even the Queen would be there! Simon closed his eyes and imagined the great hall, the royal audience, and himself standing alone in the spotlight. His stomach gurgled harder. Tonight would be rehearsal - the performance would be in just a few days. Barklee, his best friend and traveling companion, was not nervous at all. She nestled in her seat with her nose pressed against the window.

Their first glimpse of the island was of rolling green countryside sprinkled with rivers and roads. Villages and towns with red-roofed houses drew closer and closer as the plane settled down for a smooth landing at Heathrow International Airport.

As they left the plane, Simon & Barklee looked around for their guide. He was to meet them by the baggage claim. Suddenly, they heard a booming voice.

"Simon! Barklee! Over here!" They looked through the crowds. There he was. Sir Nigel Bridgeton-Smythe, a large and shaggy sheepdog, waved a white hanky in their direction.

New Words

Royal Albert Hall - a famous and historic hall in London where musical concerts, plays and exhibitions are held.

"Welcome to Great Britain," Sir Nigel said as he peered at them through glasses perched unsteadily at the very end of his nose. Barklee looked up at him, puzzled. She poked Simon in the ribs.

"Simon, I thought we were in England," she said softly. "What's Great Britain?" Sir Nigel overheard her question and explained.

"Well, my dear, it is the same thing," he said as he picked up their suitcases. "Great Britain is the formal name of this island. Great Britain includes England, Scotland and Wales. Then, when you add Northern Ireland on another island nearby, the whole thing is called the United Kingdom. It can be a bit confusing. But come along now. Much to see. Much to do." With that, he headed off at a fast clip. Simon and Barklee trotted along behind.

As they hastened toward the parking lot, their host told them he planned to show them around the city of London before Simon's rehearsal that night. Barklee immediately spoke up.

"We want to go to the ***castle*** and meet the king," she said.

"Well, we do not have a king who lives in a castle," Sir Nigel said. "We have a queen who lives in a ***palace***. Buckingham Palace. Shall we go see it?" He rescued the glasses that were about to slide off the end of his nose. "England is one of the few countries that still has a ***monarchy***. Queen Elizabeth ***II*** has been our ***monarch*** for almost fifty years."

Simon and Barklee meet Sir Nigel at Heathrow.

He came to a stop in front of a small, red Morris motorcar, yanked open the doors and loaded everyone inside.

"Excuse me, Sir Nigel, but the car doesn't have a top," said Barklee. "Won't we get wet? I read in our guidebook that it rains quite a lot in England."

"Not to worry," Sir Nigel told her. I never get wet. I carry a ***brolly*** in the ***boot***."

He started the engine, and with a jerk and a sputter they were off.

As they pulled out of the parking lot, Simon's neck feathers suddenly shot straight out. "Sir Nigel!" he shrieked. "You're driving on the wrong side of the road!"

The sheepdog smiled calmly and pushed his glasses higher on his nose. He steered with one hand as he patted Simon's feathers.

"Not at all, lad. Not at all," he said. "We drive on the other side here. Look at the steering wheel. You see? It is on the right side of the car. And we drive on the left side of the road. Mind you now," he cautioned, "while you are here, always look to the right before stepping into a road. Cars always come from the right - not from the left as they do in your home town. 'Check right,' I always say."

New Words

castle - a large fortress or group of buildings with thick walls, battlements, and sometimes a moat.

palace - a large, magnificent building that is the residence of kings and queens.

monarchy - a government or a country that is headed by a king or queen.

II - the Roman numeral for "2" or "the second".

monarch - the ruler of a country, a king or queen.

brolly - what Londoners call an umbrella.

boot - what the English call the trunk of a car.

Oh, no! They are driving on the wrong side!

The Palace and Parliament

Sir Nigel threaded the car through heavy London traffic towards Buckingham Palace. It was not long before the visitors looked in astonishment at the grand building that had been home of England's kings and queens for many years. They stared at the world famous ***Welsh Guards***, standing straight and tall at full attention in front of each of the palace gates. Each wore a splendid uniform with a tall bearskin hat.

"They never move," Sir Nigel told them. "While the guards are on duty, they stand absolutely still. Lots of tourists try to make them laugh, but the guards never do."

Barklee decided to try. She borrowed a souvenir bearskin hat from a tourist standing nearby, plopped it on her head, and pranced over to stand beside one of the motionless guards. She stuck out her tongue and began to dance a funny little jig. Simon and Sir Nigel laughed at her ***antics***, but the guard never moved. He stood just like a statue. Barklee wondered if he was real.

Simon nearly jumped out of his feathers when the guard suddenly stamped his foot and began to march to the sound of horns and drums. The ***Changing of the Guards Ceremony*** had begun. Hundreds of tourists lined the streets as guards on horseback paraded to the palace gates. The guards saluted as fresh troops replaced the old.

New Words

Welsh Guards - famous guards of Buckingham Palace. "Welsh" means from the part of the Great Britain called Wales.

antics - playful and silly behavior.

Changing of the Guards Ceremony - every day at 11:00 guards in magnificent uniforms ride horses and march down the avenue toward the palace to take their places and stand guard over the palace gates.

The guards stand like statues.

The visitors left the palace and headed into the center of the city. Traffic swirled around as the old car rattled and banged its way along the busy streets. Sir Nigel pointed left and right, talking nonstop. His glasses slipped and slid, this way and that, until finally he perched them on top of his head. He turned to look at his new friends.

"Have you any ***pounds***?" he asked, squinting at them.

Barklee looked at him strangely. "Pounds of what?" she asked.

"Not pounds of anything. It is what English money is called. It used to mean pounds of sterlings - meaning silver coins, but now it is just paper money called pounds. And 100 ***pence*** make a pound. If you want to buy souvenirs or eat in restaurants, you will have to have pounds." Sir Nigel stopped at a bank and they exchanged some dollars for the English money.

The visitors looked at the unfamiliar coins and bills turning them over and over. They thought it was fun to have a new kind of money to spend as they counted their pounds and pence. Barklee bought some postcards, then put the money away carefully as Sir Nigel drove on through the city.

"Look there, Simon," he said. "I am sure you recognize that famous building." They were in front of the pointed arches and tall spires of the ***Houses of Parliament*** along the banks of the ***River Thames***. "That is where England's lawmakers work."

Big Ben chimes the hours.

Simon and Barklee gazed with awe at the mighty towers. One of them held Big Ben, a nickname for the best-known bell in the kingdom. "Most people think Big Ben is the name of the clock," Sir Nigel told them. "When it was first hung there about 150 years ago, it meant just the bell. Now Big Ben means the whole tower. It is 103 meters tall."

Simon, who had learned the metric system, said, "Barklee, that means 320 feet tall. One meter is the same as 39.37 inches. You just have to do the math."

Suddenly, they heard a mighty BONG! Big Ben was sounding the hour. Sir Nigel said, "The bell weighs 11,793 kilos." He turned to Barklee with a grin. "One kilo is the same as 2.2 pounds. How much is that, Barklee?"

She crossed her eyes and thought. "Real heavy," she replied.

Across from Parliament the visitors entered a beautiful, old stone cathedral - the famous Westminster Abbey. "This is where our kings and queens are crowned," Sir Nigel explained as they walked under the ***vaulted*** roof. "Some of our monarchs are buried here."

"Where?" asked Barklee in surprise. "Right under your feet," he replied. Barklee jumped back to look. Sure enough, there were stone slabs in the floor with names carved in them. Others were buried in the walls. The church was filled with 700 years of English history.

New Words

pounds - money of Great Britain, both bills and coins. Its symbol looks like this: £

pence - coins of Great Britain. 100 of them make one pound.

Houses of Parliament - a magnificent building hundreds of years old, where the English lawmakers meet.

River Thames - pronounced "TEMS," the river runs through the middle of the city of London.

vaulted - an arched roof or ceiling.

The Tower of London

"Now, where are my spectacles?" said Sir Nigel to himself as they came out onto the street again, headed for the car. A ***bobby*** on a bicycle heard him and stopped to help look for them.

Simon tapped Sir Nigel on the shoulder. "I think they're on top of your head," he said. There they were, perched high on his forehead.

The bobby looked at Sir Nigel carefully. "Excuse me, sir," he said. "Perhaps it would be best to show your guests the sights on foot. It is a good idea to see London from the ***pavement***, especially when wearing your spectacles on top of your head."

"Jolly good plan," said Sir Nigel. A minute later, the three were headed down the street with Sir Nigel in the lead. He began to sing as they wound their way through the crowds.

"London Bridge is falling down,
Falling down, falling down.
London Bridge is falling down..."

"It is?" Barklee asked. "Oh, good. Let's go watch!"

Soon, the three were looking at the famous London Bridge itself. A stiff breeze blew as the waters of the River Thames rolled beneath the bridge.

"Well, as you can see," said Sir Nigel, "it is not falling down. The bridge in the nursery rhyme was an old wooden bridge that stood here a thousand years ago. That one did fall down. We are looking at the fourth London Bridge. Many people are confused about what London Bridge looks like. They confuse it with the famous Tower Bridge. Now, look over there, my young friends," he said, pointing down river. "On the left shore we shall find the story of the best and worst of my city. We are going to the Tower of London. And see there? There is the Tower Bridge, too."

Simon and Barklee knew that it was more than just a tower. Several famous buildings stood together inside the walls of the large fortress. It was built on ruins left by the Romans almost 2,000 years ago, and parts of it still standing are 1,000 years old.

"Years ago, ***royals*** lived in the tower," Sir Nigel explained. "Then it became a prison."

"A thousand years old?" Simon said. "Wow. There aren't any buildings that old at home."

London Bridge is not falling down.

As the three visitors walked across an ancient drawbridge, they were met by a smiling gentleman wearing a fine red and black uniform, a black hat, and sparkling white gloves. "Welcome to the Tower of London," he said. "I am a ***Beefeater*** and I will be your guide."

Beefeaters guide visitors at the Tower of London.

Barklee looked at him, surprised. "I am a beef-eater, too," she stated. "I eat beef most of the time."

The guide chuckled and said, "The word Beefeater is a nickname. Our real title is Yeoman Warder of the Tower. Forty Beefeaters live here and guard the buildings and grounds. Our job is to explain the Tower's history to visitors. And yes, Beefeaters sometimes eat beef." he added.

New Words

bobby - what policemen are called in London.

pavement - what sidewalks are called in England.

royals - another word for kings and queens and members of their families.

Beefeaters - the nickname for guards at the Tower of London.

Simon and Barklee learned that a Beefeater's biggest responsibility is guarding the crown jewels, the precious gems the Queen and members of the royal family wear on special occasions. "Most of the time," the Beefeater explained, "the treasures are displayed under lock and key in the ***Duke of Wellington's Barracks***."

Their guide led the visitors inside where they ***ogled*** the fabulous royal jewels.

Both Simon and Barklee were at a loss for words. They couldn't believe their eyes when they spied the royal ***scepter***. Fashioned like a walking stick, the top of the scepter was set with a piece of the biggest diamond ever found. It was as big as both of Barklee's paws held together.

A crown of pure gold captured her imagination. She could just imagine how splendid she would look wearing it. There was a second crown, made with 3,000 diamonds, worn by the Queen when she carries the royal scepter. The Beefeater explained that the Queen must sit a lot when she wears the diamond crown because the gold and jewels are very heavy. They learned that diamonds are valued in units of weight called ***carats***.

Queen Barklee.

New Words

Duke of Wellington's Barracks - a building inside the Tower of London where the crown jewels are kept.

ogled - stared.

scepter - a rod or staff that is held by kings and queens during ceremonies.

carats - a unit of weight for precious jewels. It is the same as 200 milligrams.

"Come, let us go to the White Tower," exclaimed the Beefeater, setting off quickly. "It is the oldest part of the Tower of London fortress, built in 1078. It is filled with bows and arrows, lances and swords, shields and suits of armor - all the weapons of soldiers and knights who lived and fought hundreds of years ago. You will enjoy that." The visitors trotted along after him, amazed at the different kinds of armor. Simon daydreamed of knights on horseback who ***jousted*** with lances. Barklee wondered if the suits of armor creaked when they got rusty from the rain.

Still lost in daydreams, the visitors followed their guide to the Bloody Tower, which once was a prison.

"Centuries ago, many Londoners were sent to the Bloody Tower and never came back," said the Beefeater. "Some of the prisoners who lived and died here were victims of the famous ***King Henry VIII***. He beheaded one of his six wives and at least fifty men he thought were his enemies. The axe fell on them at Tower Hill, near this terrible prison. They were held here until they met their fate." The visitors fell silent, imagining the Bloody Tower's dark past.

Lost in a dream of centuries gone by, Simon's thoughts wandered into a shadowy tower hallway. Something mysterious drew him deeper into the gloom. He drifted down one dismal corridor and then another. In his mind he saw the iron bars that had jailed the prisoners long ago.

Suddenly, he thought he heard a hoarse voice whisper in his ear.

"You should not have come here!"

"Wha . .what? Who said that?" He almost jumped out of his feathers.

A single candle was the only light in the dim, damp prison. All at once, a whiff of cold air snuffed it out. Simon was in total darkness.

"You have ***trespassed***. Now you must pay the price."

"Price? What kind of price?" he croaked.

"We must remove a head!"

"Remove a head?" he gasped.

"Yes, remove a head. Move over here so we can axe it, Simon."

He shook his head hard. "How do you know my name is Simon?"

"Because I'm your best friend, you silly bird. You've been daydreaming again." Barklee's voice snapped him out of his daydream. She pushed him along impatiently. "Move ahead so we can exit."

Simon sighed in relief. He was the kind of bird who had a strong imagination. Now and then he heard and saw things others did not, and sometimes they were scary.

The Beefeater led the way back into the courtyard. He pointed to six large black birds that were picking at grass seeds in the lawn below the drawbridge. "Ravens," he said. "They are the most lasting residents of the tower. Their croaking cries have been heard here longer than anyone can remember."

He told them the legend of the ravens. "It is said that the city of London will fall if the birds leave. To make sure they do not fly away, their wing feathers are clipped. When one of them dies, it is replaced with a young bird so there will always be six." Simon was horrified at the thought of clipped wings.

New Words

joust - a warlike game between knights on horseback. They carried long lances, or spears, and tried to knock each other off their horses.

King Henry VIII - King of England from 1509-1547. The VIII is the Roman numeral for "8" or "the eighth."

trespass - to enter a place unlawfully.

Simon does not like the thought of clipped wings.

An English Tradition

It was afternoon when they left the tower. Simon felt nervous again, thinking about his rehearsal that evening. He was hungry and knew that a bird cannot sing sweetly on an empty stomach. Barklee, too, was ready for a bite.

"I have it!" Sir Nigel exclaimed. "We will go straight away to my favorite ***pub!*** It is quite near Piccadilly Circus." Quickly, he brought the Morris around and drove his young friends back toward the center of the city.

"Sir Nigel, will we get to see elephants and camels and clowns at Piccadilly Circus?" asked Barklee excitedly.

"No," he said with a laugh. "In England, a 'circus' means something very different. Here, it is simply a circle where several streets come together. But I must say, traffic circles are great fun." With a big "Woof!" he swooped into a merry-go-round of cars, buses and taxis winding around and around a statue in the middle of the circle.

Sir Nigel pulled to a stop in front of the *Sniff 'N' Scratch* pub. It was a ***quaint***, cozy building with old timbered walls, heavy wooden doors, and a funny sign hanging outside.

"***Bangers and mash*** for three, ***Guv'nor***," Sir Nigel called to the innkeeper.

The light inside was low. Dark wooden beams stretched all the way across the low ceiling. A big stone fireplace in one corner held a shield with crossed swords over the mantle.

"Pubs are an important part of life in Great Britain," Sir Nigel said. "In small villages and in large cities, they are meeting places where friends gather for food, games and conversation."

Barklee was happy to sit down for a while. She was puzzled and had an important question.

"Sir Nigel, why is your first name 'Sir'? Is it an English name?"

He smiled and said, "Well, my dear, it is not my first name. It is a title. It means that I am a ***knight***."

The two visitors gasped. "A knight!" they chorused. "Really? You're a knight?"

"Do you have a suit of armor like we saw at the Tower of London?" Barklee asked.

"No, no armor. Not in these days. But I truly am a Knight of the ***Realm***.

English pubs are filled with good cheer.

For many years, I served our Queen in foreign lands. I was the Captain of the Guards of the Queens Own Canines. Once or twice we got into scrapes and I had to rescue some chaps. The Queen made me a knight for bravery." He winked at Barklee and said, "Girls can be knights, too. They are given the title of 'Dame'." Barklee's mind took off in a daydream. *Imagine!* she thought. *Dame Barklee!*

"Now let us eat," said Sir Nigel. "Then we will have a game of darts before we leave for the concert hall." They went to work on their steaming plates of grilled sausages and mashed potatoes.

Simon was feeling jittery about the upcoming rehearsal, so after lunch he watched while Barklee played darts with Sir Nigel. She even hit the target with two of them. But poor Sir Nigel! His glasses had slid sideways again and were dangling from one ear. His first few darts hit the wall behind a nearby table, badly frightening the customers having lunch there.

The two played happily for some time while Simon thought and worried. As the shadows lengthened, Sir Nigel gathered the visitors in the Morris and they departed for the Royal Albert Hall and Simon's rehearsal.

New Words

pub - a "public house". In England, they are places where people gather to visit, eat and drink.

quaint - pleasingly old-fashioned.

bangers and mash - an English dish of sausages and mashed potatoes.

Guv'nor - a slang word used in London. It means "boss".

knight - in olden days, a servant of a king. Now it is a title awarded by the British monarchy to people of high achievement.

realm - another word for kingdom.

Simon & Barklee
in England

Rehearsal

It was not long before they pulled up before a magnificent, domed building. Simon ***gawked*** at it, thunderstruck. His throat was suddenly dry.

Sir Nigel spoke up. "Here we are, my friends. We Englanders call this the Nation's Village Hall. One hundred fifty years ago, Albert, who was the husband of Queen Victoria, built the hall as a ***cultural center***. Many performances take place here: music, dance, plays and more. Shall we go in?" With that, he led them right inside to the stage.

Simon walked slowly to the middle of the stage and turned to face the empty seats. He looked at Sir Nigel and Barklee sitting in the first row. His stomach lurched. He took a deep breath, opened his mouth, and out came... *nothing*. He cleared his throat and tried again. This time he managed a squeak. Then a squawk. He was so nervous that he could not make one single note sound right.

Barklee looked up at her friend and saw how worried he was. She jumped onto the stage and put her paws on his shoulders and spoke to him quietly. "Simon, you musn't be worried. You're a wonderful singer. You're just feeling nervous right now. It's all right. Everyone gets nervous before a performance, especially one that's for the Queen! I think we should just relax and have a few days of fun. Then, when it's time for the real show, you'll be just wonderful. You're the best, you know."

Sir Nigel understood that Simon had developed an early case of stage fright. "We will see a bit of the country first, then when we come back to London you will be in ***fine fettle*** again." Simon took a deep, shaky breath, swallowed the lump in his throat, and agreed.

New Words

gawk - to stare in a stupid way.

cultural center - a place people go to improve their minds, to learn and appreciate new things.

fine fettle - an expression that means "at your best".

Simon has stage fright.

An Ancient Mystery

Early the next morning, Sir Nigel collected the travelers, jumped into the old Morris and headed out of the city. Simon and Barklee giggled when they saw that he had carefully tied his eyeglasses to his ears with pieces of yarn, hoping they would stay in place.

As the old Morris sputtered along the ***motorway***, Sir Nigel asked, "By the by, do you like puzzles?"

"You bet," said Simon.

"I don't know," Barklee replied. "Puzzles are a mystery to me."

"Well then," Sir Nigel promised, "in a little while you will see a giant mystery that has remained unsolved for almost four thousand years. ***Stonehenge***." Four thousand years! Neither Simon nor Barklee could imagine anything - even a mystery - lasting that long. "Did the world even exist then?" Barklee asked Simon.

Sir Nigel's eyeglasses slipped again. The yarn had unraveled and the spectacles dangled dangerously from one ear. Simon gulped in alarm as the old Morris motorcar began to weave dangerously along the road.

Barklee decided to solve the problem. She tugged on Sir Nigel's sleeve and pleaded, "May I drive? I know how - even on the wrong side of the road. I promise to check right at every corner," she added. Simon turned pale.

"Very well," Sir Nigel said. He stopped long enough to scoot over and let her take the wheel. "Off we go then, to see the mystery of Stonehenge. Remember your promise, Barklee. Check right!"

"Check!" said Barklee.

"Oh, dear!" said Simon.

As they zipped along the country roads, Sir Nigel called out, "Mind the ***roundabout***!"

"Round about what?" Barklee called back.

"The traffic circle coming up," said Sir Nigel.

"Check right!" shouted Sir Nigel and Simon together.

Barklee swooped into the circle so tightly that the old car scraped the curb.

"Oh, m'gosh!" Simon yelled. "Someone is throwing Frisbees at us!"

Barklee discovers roundabouts.

"Not Frisbees, lad" Sir Nigel yelled back. "Those are my ***wheel covers***!"

Barklee quickly got the car back under control. She aimed straight down the lane. Simon helped Sir Nigel find his eyeglasses that had flown off during Barklee's madcap whirl through the roundabout.

With Simon holding on to Sir Nigel, and Sir Nigel holding on for dear life, Barklee finally brought the Morris to a rattling stop. They were on the Salisbury Plain, a wide-open space in the southern part of England, west of London.

New Words

motorway - the English word for freeway.

Stonehenge - a famous and ancient stone circle on the Salisbury Plain in southern England. It was built by prehistoric people. No one really knows what it was for.

roundabout - what a traffic circle is called in England.

wheel covers - what hubcaps are called in England.

No one was there except the three travelers. The ancient stones stood silently in front of them - a circle in an empty field. Some stood in pairs, with huge stones lying across their tops. Others stood alone, silent as ***sentinels***. Some lay scattered in a circle on the ground. Not a sound broke the stillness as they stared at the mysterious stone circle. It took several minutes for Simon to find his voice.

"How did they get here?" he asked in a hushed tone.

"That is the big mystery," said Sir Nigel. "No one really knows. These stones have stood silently on this plain for four thousand years. Just imagine. Stonehenge was here long before London - long before any of our ancestors came: the Celts, or the Romans, or the Vikings, or the Saxons or Normans. Only a few people lived on this island then. There were no towns or roads. Just a few villages - and the stones. Some think it was a temple, others say an ***observatory***."

As Sir Nigel's voice died away, the sun emerged from under a bank of clouds, casting a reddish glow against the towering stones. Deep shadows lay on the ground beneath them. Barklee wandered into the mysterious circle, stopping here and there to look upward at its height against the sky. She could feel the power of those old stones and the mystery of their ancient builders. She shivered a little and returned to stand beside Simon.

"There are other prehistoric stone circles in Great Britain, but this one is the biggest," Sir Nigel continued.

"But how did it get built?" Simon asked. "Prehistoric people didn't have cranes and machinery to lift these huge stones into place. Who put them there? And where did they come from? They must weight 8,000 pounds apiece!" Simon was fascinated. He looked all around. There were no cliffs or rocky hills nearby where the stones might have come from.

Sir Nigel replied, "There are many ideas about how they came to be here. Some people believe aliens from outer space arrived in spaceships and built Stonehenge."

The idea of aliens captured Barklee's fancy. "Martians," she announced. "It must have been Martians. They came here and built an airport for their flying saucers."

Simon shook his head and smiled at her imagination.

As they walked among the ruins, Sir Nigel told them the stones represented an intelligent design from prehistoric times. He thought he knew how the stones had been brought to the empty plain.

"It is only a guess," he said, "but I think long poles were made from trees and then laid side by side in a row on the ground. Stones from far away were pulled over the poles by oxen. Of course, there were no ***lorries*** in those days. The big mystery is how they got the stones to stand up and not fall down. Can you imagine how hard it would be with no machinery and very few tools?"

Stonehenge is a four-thousand year-old mystery.

The visit to the ancient stones had put Simon in a ***pensive*** mood. He thought about England and the people who had lived on the island through the centuries.

"Just think," he said out loud. "People have been living here for thousands of years. This small country has a long and wonderful history."

New Words

sentinel - a guard.

observatory - a building for studying the stars.

lorries - what trucks are called in England.

pensive - thoughtful or dreamy.

The Bard

They took to the open winding road again - the sheepdog, the terrier and the canary - headed north. Sir Nigel had promised them a peek into another famous place.

"Anyone for a bit of Shakespeare?" Sir Nigel asked.

"Shake what?" Barklee said.

"Shakespeare," Sir Nigel repeated, "a bit of Shakespeare."

"Sir Nigel means William Shakespeare," Simon said. "He wrote many famous plays in Old English, with funny words like '***forsooth***' and '***methinks***'."

"It sounds funny to us now," Sir Nigel observed, "but that is the way English was spoken three hundred years ago. Since then, actors speaking olden-day English have delighted audiences all over the world, reciting Shakespeare's famous lines. He lived and wrote in a ***hamlet*** not far from here, called Stratford-upon-Avon. Many visitors go there every year. Shall we?"

"Forsooth!" said Simon.

"Check right!" said Barklee.

They found Stratford-upon-Avon on the banks of the Avon River, in the middle of England. Old houses made of stone and heavy timbers lined the streets.

Sir Nigel explained why so many houses in England are made of stone. "The soil in England used to be full of them. People needed to clear the land for planting, so they dug up the stones and used them to build houses. Roofs of many houses were covered with thatch, made of thick batches of straw. It made good, sturdy roofs that did not leak. But sometimes birds nested in the thatch. Or plants, even trees, started growing right there on the roofs!"

Simon noticed that everything in Stratford-upon-Avon had something to do with William Shakespeare. Sir Nigel pointed to a double house on Henley Street and said, "There, friends, is where the old ***bard*** was born."

"The old what?" Barklee asked, cocking her head.

"Bard. A bard is someone who writes and sings."

They stepped inside the house where Shakespeare lived and wrote some of his plays. "Only gifted actors and actresses perform Shakespeare," said Sir Nigel.

Shakespeare's home town.

"The lines in Old English are difficult to recite. The most famous of all Shakespearean theaters is right here in Stratford."

Simon's eyes lit up. He turned to Barklee and reminded her that he knew a few of Shakespeare's plays and verses.

"I'd like to recite some lines in the theater. Let's go look for it," he said. The two took off down the street, calling for Sir Nigel to follow them.

"On my way," Sir Nigel called. He huffed along behind them, pushing and pulling at his spectacles with each step.

The two visitors found the theater closed. Simon, however, was not discouraged. He flew around the building until he found a partly opened window. They climbed inside. Barklee held on to Simon's tail feathers as they crept down the aisle of the empty theater.

"This is nutty, Simon," Barklee whispered. "We'll probably get in trouble for sneaking in here."

But Simon was not listening. He poked around until he found a switch that lighted center stage. He stood in the circle of light, and stared at the floor as though deep in thought. Then, as he held one wing across his breast and pointed to the ceiling with the other, he raised his head and recited in a strong voice:

"*Friends, Romans, countrymen, lend me your ears...*"

Barklee broke into a fit of giggles. Imagine, borrowing someone's ears!

"*I come to bury Caesar, not to praise him.*

The evil that men do lives after them,

The good is oft interred with their bones."

"That was from Shakespeare's play 'Julius Caesar,' Barklee," said Simon "Now listen. This line is from 'Romeo and Juliet'. Pay attention."

"Romeo, Romeo. Wherefore art thou, Romeo?"

"Well, he's not here, Simon. Let's get out of here before someone catches us," Barklee urged.

But Simon continued until, suddenly, all the lights came on. The two of them heard shouts of "Bravo! Bravo!" coming from the back of the theater. Sir Nigel stood with of a group of people who wore costumes from 300 years ago. They were the famous Shakespearean actors of Stratford-upon-Avon! They applauded mightily until Simon took several bows and finally fluttered off the stage. Barklee and Sir Nigel beamed. Simon felt a bit better about being on stage. The memory of the awful rehearsal in London began to fade away.

New Words

forsooth and methinks - old English words no longer used. They mean "indeed, no doubt" and "I think."

hamlet - a small village.

bard - a poet, or sometimes a singer who played the harp.

Simon performs one of Shakespeare's most famous scenes.

An Adventure in the Hedgerows

"Jolly good show, dear boy!" Sir Nigel woofed as they putt-putted out of Stratford-upon-Avon. "I particularly liked the verse from 'Julius Caesar.' Do you know who Caesar was, Barklee?"

"Of course I do. He invented Caesar salad," she replied.

Sir Nigel barked out a huge laugh. "Julius Caesar was a very famous soldier and an emperor of Rome. An emperor is the ruler of an empire, and Rome was the largest empire in the world two thousand years ago. Parts of it covered even England. I want you to see something amazing that the Romans built. It is called Hadrian's Wall. At one time it stretched across all of England.

"On our way, we will stay the night on a farm," Sir Nigel added. "It is called a ***bed and breakfast*** inn. It is a fine way to meet the people of England and enjoy the countryside." He pointed the Morris north and drove off with his glasses planted firmly on top of his head.

It was not long before Floyd and Mildred Duckworth, owners of *Birds of a Feather Farm*, welcomed them at the gate of their inn with a basket of freshly baked treats.

"Oh, do come in and have some fresh ***scones***," Mrs. Duckworth invited. "I have put fresh blackberries in them. And here are some sweet butter and homemade jam." She sat them down and brought out pots of hot cocoa and tea. Simon, Barklee and Sir Nigel were soon sticky with butter and jam.

New Words

bed and breakfast - a small inn or private home where travelers can spend a comfortable night. A big breakfast is served in the morning.

scones - a delicious baked treat from England that is somewhat like a biscuit.

Welcome to Birds of a Feather farm.

"There is a lot to see on an English farm, my young friends. Why not explore a bit before dinner?" Mildred Duckworth suggested. Simon and Barklee promptly shot out the door.

Soon they found an old cobblestone bridge that cast a wiggly shadow on the running water below. They paused to throw a few stones, then raced off into a nearby field to scatter grazing sheep. They had such fun that they did not watch where they ran. All at once, they spied a bad-tempered ram. It started toward them, head down and horns up.

"Uh, oh!" Barklee warned. "We're in for it now!"

They quickly looked for a haystack or a tree to climb. Nothing.

"Run, Barklee! Run!" Simon yelled, as he took wing and flew out of the ram's path. Barklee made a beeline for a ***hedgerow*** across the pasture and ducked into the first opening she saw. Panting, she squeezed under the thick vines and brush and pushed herself in as far as she could wiggle. The ram snorted and pawed the ground, but he could not reach her. She was safe.... for the moment.

Simon had flown far from the field and could not remember which one they had been in. There were sheep in all of them. He did not see Barklee anywhere. Worried, he flew back to the farmhouse to find help.

Barklee quickly learned about English hedgerows. She was firmly tangled and could not move. It seemed the more she struggled, the tighter the vines held her. She was stuck and out of luck.

Or so it seemed.

New Words

hedgerow - a row of bushes that grow together to make a fence. Many of the hedgerows in England are hundreds of years old.

Barklee runs to safety in a hedgerow.

"Need help, do you?" A fox suddenly appeared at Barklee's side. "Please, allow me to help," it said. "Foxes know all about hedgerows. We spend a lot of time in them, hiding from hunters." The fox pulled at some thorns that were wrapped around Barklee's ears.

"Say, fellows," he called out. "Come give us a hand." Within moments, rabbits, squirrels and a grouse had appeared. They tut-tutted and clucked and sniffed as they helped the fox untangle Barklee's ears and tail from the fierce thorns. As they worked, they told her stories of life in the hedgerows. They said their great-great grandparents had lived in that very place so many years ago. Barklee learned that the hedgerows of England were so old and ***dense*** that farmers did not need fences. She also discovered that they were home to ***generations*** of small animals.

As the hedgerow ***residents*** removed the last of the thorns and brambles, Barklee wriggled from her trap. With a sigh of relief, she turned to thank her rescuers. She peered around, ears twitching to sense danger, but the angry ram had disappeared.

A loud popping noise suddenly filled the air, and the fox and his friends vanished in a flash. It was Floyd Duckworth, with Sir Nigel and Simon on his tractor, chugging towards her through the field. Barklee was covered in stickers and leaves and looked thoroughly ***bedraggled***. Climbing onto the back of Floyd's tractor, she settled down as they rode off to the farmhouse.

They were starved when they arrived. Mildred had prepared a good hot supper of roast beef and Yorkshire pudding.

"Pudding for dinner?" asked Barklee. "We never get to eat dessert first at home."

"Not like the pudding you are used to, I expect," Mildred explained as she filled their plates. "This one is made of eggs, flour and milk, and baked in the drippings from a roast. It is a very famous dish in England." When it came time for the real dessert, she asked if anyone would like a big slice of gooseberry pie, topped with a layer of thick cream. Two wings and four paws shot straight up.

The evening log popped merrily in the parlor fireplace. Simon and Barklee sprawled on a rug, pillows under their heads, and stared dreamily into the flames. After such a busy day, it was difficult to stay awake. They soon made their way to their bedrooms and fell fast asleep.

A relaxing end to a day of adventure.

New Words

dense - very thick.

resident - a person who lives in a place.

bedraggled - wet, limp and dirty.

generation - the average span of time between the birth of parents and that of their children.

In the morning, the travelers skipped downstairs and discovered a typical English breakfast of ham, eggs, mushrooms, tomatoes and slices of bread - all cooked together in the same pan at the same time. *Any more food and I will be as fat as an owl,* Simon thought.

Mildred Duckworth packed a nice picnic lunch for their journey while Floyd gave Sir Nigel directions north towards Hadrian's Wall.

"Now, you follow the lanes north to the towns of Stoke-on-Trent, Bradford and Carlisle. The roads are a bit hilly in places and curvy, too. You will pass lots of villages. But mind you, if you get to Barfing-on-Berber you've gone too far!" he said.

Simon and Barklee looked at each other and broke into fits of giggles when they heard that.

Simon & Barklee
in England

The Romans in England

The old Morris bounced along roads where Roman soldiers had marched two thousand years before. As they traveled, Sir Nigel told the story. "Hadrian's Wall was built by ***Roman Emperor Hadrian*** about one hundred years after Julius Caesar left England. It was ***117 kilometers*** long across the narrow neck of England, from the North Sea to the Irish Sea. The Romans built it because they were afraid that the people of the north might attack them."

While Sir Nigel parked, Simon and Barklee hopped out and walked slowly towards the silent, ghostly remains of the crumbling wall. Grayish-green moss was growing on the stones and little sprigs of grass poked out of the cracks. Fog drifted silently along the remains of the ancient wall. They thought of the five hundred soldiers who once lived and worked right where they were standing.

Simon, wandering off alone, pictured himself as a Roman ***centurion***. He wondered what life was like for the soldiers of that long-ago time. As he walked, he spied something shiny partly buried in the dirt and pried it out with his foot. It was an ancient coin, with a man's head on one side, a building on the other. Carefully, he picked it up and brushed the dirt from its surface. He gazed at it in wonder.

"I bet this was lost by a Roman soldier," Simon said to himself.

"It was. I lost it."

Stunned, Simon whirled around. There, standing amid the fog and the ruins, was the image of a handsome, young Roman soldier. He had a kind face and spoke softly.

"I am - or was - Marcus Larium, a junior officer in a British legion assigned to defend this part of the wall."

Simon stood absolutely still while the soldier explained that the coin had special meaning. He said Emperor Hadrian personally gave it to him in the days when the wall was new.

"Do you like to read?" Marcus Larium asked.

"Oh, I read all the time," Simon replied, thinking it was an odd question.

"I was born and raised near this wall and I am standing exactly where my *ludus* was," the soldier said. "We spoke the ancient language of Latin, and *ludus* is Latin for primary school. This is where I learned to read and write." He explained that paper had not been invented then, so he wrote on tablets coated with wax. Later, he read from scrolls made of papyrus, which were made from Egyptian reeds.

"When I was eleven, I attended *grammaticus*, what you call middle school. I studied subjects like history, geography and astronomy and art. I liked reading about Greece, especially. Greek culture had a big influence on Roman life…even here in ***Britannia***."

Simon meets the ghost of Marcus Larium.

"You studied Greek when you were eleven?" Simon asked in disbelief.

"Quite so," the soldier responded. "Most of my teachers were Greek slaves who spoke Latin. They were brought here as educators. The finest books were written by Greeks, so it was important to learn that language. Some of my friends even went to Greece to study. They became lawyers and politicians."

Simon was enthralled.

"What is your favorite subject to study?" Marcus Larium asked.

"Music. I love opera and I want to sing from the great stages of the world. Do you like music?"

"I enjoy the sweet notes of the ***lyre*** and the flute," the soldier replied. "Music soothes my warrior soul."

"Is - I mean was - there anything you didn't like here?" said Simon.

"The cold," Marcus Larium answered. "I nearly froze while standing winter watch on top of Hadrian's Wall. Even the woolen cloak and trousers I wore and my wood and leather shield were no protection against the blasts of icy winds."

Simon shivered.

"Thank you for finding my coin. After looking for so many years, I am happy to have it returned. It has been a long and frustrating search, but Romans learned long ago not to get discouraged when something we tried to do was difficult. Our lives were often hard, but we were very strong and brave."

New Words

Roman Emperor Hadrian - emperor of Rome from 117-138 AD, almost 2,000 years ago.

117 kilometers - metric measurement about the same as 73 miles. One mile is 1.60 kilometers.

centurion - an officer in the army of ancient Rome.

Britannia - what England was called by the Romans.

lyre - a small stringed instrument rather like a harp.

Simon thought about that. He looked down at his feet and remembered the failed rehearsal at the Royal Albert Hall. It had been very hard. He thought about the life of Marcus Larium and the soldiers of the wall. Their lives, too, were hard, but they did not give up. Suddenly, he was filled with confidence. He knew that his performance back in London would be spectacular. The spirit of Marcus Larium would stay with him.

"Hey, Simon!" Simon turned at the sudden sound of Barklee's voice.

"C'mon down, Simon." Barklee waved her paws and skipped around on flat rocks in a shallow dip in the ground. "We can take a bath." She stood in the ruins of a bathhouse for soldiers.

Simon whirled and looked back toward the ludus. Marcus Larium had vanished.

The coin that had lain at Simon's feet was gone, too. *Was he real?* Simon wondered. *Was it another daydream?* He shook his feathers, took a deep breath, then smiled. Whichever it was, he felt fine. He jumped down to meet Barklee.

Sir Nigel pointed to holes where bath water used to come in and go out. Next to the bathhouse, old broken bricks and stones formed a map on the ground. They could see where houses and shops once stood. The sheepdog knelt on the ground and pointed to the outlines to show how rooms might have been laid out.

"Roman engineers built excellent roads, too," he told them. "They built them throughout all their empire so they could move large armies quickly. Many of England's roads today are built where Roman roads once ran. Not far from here, you can still see the ruins of some of the ancient roadways."

Simon thought quietly about the life of long ago. Marcus Larium had taught him something about bravery. He would not forget.

An Accident in the Lake District

Their explorations ended as Sir Nigel called, "Look here, dear friends. The time has come to start back to London. The concert is just two days away. We are going to make a stop in the Lake District on the way. Hurry along now."

Once again the trio took to the road, this time heading south toward the famous Lake District of England where visitors explore, fish, boat and hike. They soon arrived in the small village of Ambleside, on the lake called Windermere. There they stopped to explore and take a small boat out on the lake. Sir Nigel was at the oars, his spectacles wobbling ***precariously***.

As they slowly made their way toward the center of the lake, a sudden gust of wind blew Sir Nigel's hanky into the water. "***Blimey***," he exclaimed. He leaned w-a-a-y out to reach it and promptly fell overboard with a mighty splash.

"SIR NIGEL!" Simon and Barklee shrieked together. A very surprised sheepdog ***thrashed*** to the surface. His glasses dangled from one ear, and his hanky floated nearby.

New Words

precariously - uncertain, insecure.

Blimey - in England, an exclamation of surprise, like "Oh, gosh!"

thrashed - in swimming, to stir about violently.

Sir Nigel takes an unexpected swim.

Simon flew off immediately to summon help as Sir Nigel called to Barklee, "I say, do throw me something to hold on to." She threw one of the oars. "I would not have suggested the oar, I think," the soggy sheepdog sputtered.

Simon quickly spotted a sturdy sheep digging in her garden behind a cottage. He landed in a flutter and told her about Sir Nigel's ***crisis***. Nodding quickly, she hurried to a shed for a long rope, then followed Simon to the dock.

What a sight! There was Barklee, frantically rowing with one oar as the boat circled around and around a bobbing Sir Nigel. Finally, he dog-paddled to the rear of the boat and held on for dear life.

"Ahoy, you drowning out there," came a bleat from the shore. "Here comes the bird with the end of a rope. I will pull you in." Simon took the end of the rope in his beak and launched out over the water to Sir Nigel's rescue. The ***ewe*** put her strong back into a hand-over-hand pull and hauled Sir Nigel, soaked and sputtering, to the shore. Barklee, now with both oars, rowed Simon to the dock.

"Come on, you," the ewe said gruffly to Sir Nigel. "You can get dry in front of my ***cooker***." She shook her head. "Imagine! A ***bloke*** falling out of a boat like that," she said.

The ewe plunked a pot of hot cocoa and tea on the table with a plate of sugar cookies. "Name is Belle," she announced. "All alone now. My husband passed on some time back. We were farmers, you see. Now I am doing the work of two. Not easy, I can tell you. Just getting by."

"Certainly there must be something we can do to repay your kindness," Sir Nigel said.

"I know what, Mrs. Belle, " Barklee exclaimed. "Sir Nigel can chop wood for the fire, and I can help with the gardening. Simon can sing happy songs that will cheer us while we work." And that is what they did. The three travelers pitched in and brightened the rescuer's day.

As evening came, Belle went inside to get supper. She soon called the three in, wiped her hands on her apron and said with a smile, "Sit down, sit down. I have made *toad-in-the-hole* to eat. Since it will be dark soon, I prepared a place in the parlor for you to sleep. No sense driving at night."

"What's in the hole, Mrs. Belle?" Barklee asked, suddenly alarmed. "A toad? You mean like a yukky frog? Are we going to eat frogs?"

Belle comes to the rescue.

"Oh, no," she answered, 'toad-in-the-hole' is what we call sausages baked in a batter. It is just the thing after a day of hard work."

"Belle," Sir Nigel said beaming, "I have a splendid solution for you. I know some young Londoners who would welcome a chance to come to the country. They would be wonderful help for you here on the farm. Count on it, Belle. I will ***ring them up*** as soon as we return to London. They will come to help you straight away."

Then, Sir Nigel blushed when she gave him a big hug.

New Words

crisis - a time of great danger.

ewe - a female sheep.

cooker - what a stove is called in England.

bloke - English slang for "a guy."

ring them up - English slang that means to telephone someone.

Simon & Barklee
in England

The Concert

The following afternoon, as the hustle and bustle of London loomed on the horizon, Sir Nigel headed for the theater. "Simon, this is your big day," he said, pushing his glasses into place once more.

In a short while the three were gazing once more at the magnificent dome of the Royal Albert Hall. Simon stood rooted to the sidewalk. He was shaking. It was time! He closed his eyes and took a deep breath. As he did, he heard a soft whisper in his mind.

Remember, my golden friend, the coin that was lost for centuries. I knew I would succeed in finding it again. So, too, will you succeed tonight. Simon straightened his feathers and raised his head. Marcus Larium's ghostly whisper restored his confidence and gave him courage.

Barklee put her arm around Simon as they walked into the Hall. "Just take a few deep breaths and pretend you're singing alone in a beautiful forest." She squeezed his shoulder and said, "You're the best, Simon." Then she joined Sir Nigel at their seats.

The audience applauded politely as the canary walked to the center of the stage. He could barely see them beyond the bright stage lights. He bowed, took a deep breath, and began.

The sweet, clear notes coming from Simon's throat were breathtaking. A single violinist swept the melody high to the domed ceiling, where the notes returned in waves down the sides of the grand hall and met in the middle. Sir Nigel thought that passersby must have wondered at the bursts of cheering from inside. Did they know that a small canary from America was enchanting his British hosts with his golden voice?

Simon finished with a melody that ended on the highest note he had ever sung. He crossed one wing across his breast and bowed deeply as the onlookers rose in applause. When the lights came on, he could see the audience and the box where the Queen and her family were seated. The Queen waved and, together with the crowd, gave Simon T. McTwill a resounding three cheers:

"Hip, hip, hooray! Hip, hip, hooray! Hip, hip, hooray!"

Simon and Barklee were ***flushed*** with excitement as they left the concert hall.

Simon sings for the Queen.

It was a splendid ending to their travels in England. Sir Nigel looked at them, a trifle sadly, and said, "I salute you for your worldwide journey. You will learn a great deal in your travels. I know this because I have traveled the world myself. We English are much like Americans in many ways, but it is interesting to discover how we are different. Can you imagine how boring life would be if we all looked, talked, and lived the same way?"

Sir Nigel urged the young travelers to visit England again. "You have not visited Canterbury and the famous cathedral. Certainly, you should visit the ***spa*** at Bath and the Roman Baths Museum. And of course, you will want to see Sulgrave Manor, the family home of your first president, George Washington. Did you know that he was born here? There is so much more to see... you will come back?"

"Of course we will, Sir Nigel," Simon promised. "You are a wonderful guide. You have made our visit here perfect."

"I loved every minute," said Barklee. " I learned a whole lot! Thank you, Sir Nigel."

As they passed through Waterloo Station, Simon and Barklee stopped at a souvenir shop to spend the rest of their English pounds and pence. They bought three woolen scarves and a box of ***treacle*** candy for the trip. They gave Sir Nigel one of the scarves to keep his neck warm, then waved and boarded the train.

On a quiet road near the edge of London, Sir Nigel sat alone in his car. His glasses tilted to one side of his large nose. He could barely see the railroad tracks, but it was not long before he heard the distant sound of a fast train approaching. The sheepdog opened the door and stood next to his old Morris, waving his new scarf as the train sped by.

Inside the train, Barklee tugged at Simon's scarf. "Look! Look!" she cried. "We're passing an old Morris car. Do you suppose it's Sir Nigel?"

As the train disappeared down the track, Sir Nigel Bridgeton-Smythe took out a large, damp hanky. He wiped a tear from his eye and blew his nose.

Farewell, we will return soon.

New Words

flush - to get red in the face.

spa - a mineral-water spring. In many European countries, a spa is a resort where people go to drink the healthful mineral water and relax.

treacle - molasses candy.

Different English Words

Biscuit - cookie
Bonnet - the hood of a car
Braces - suspenders
Chips - french fries
Cooker - stove
Crisps - chips
Flat - apartment
Lift - elevator
Loo - nickname for a bathroom
Petrol - gas
Rubbish bin - trash can
Sweets - candy
Till - a cash register
Torch - a flashlight
Tube - the London subway
Waistcoat - vest

Different English Spellings

Aeroplane - airplane
Behaviour - behavior
Colour - color
Honour - honor
Kerb - a curbing at the side of a road
Tyres - tires

Simon & Barklee say *Cheerio!*

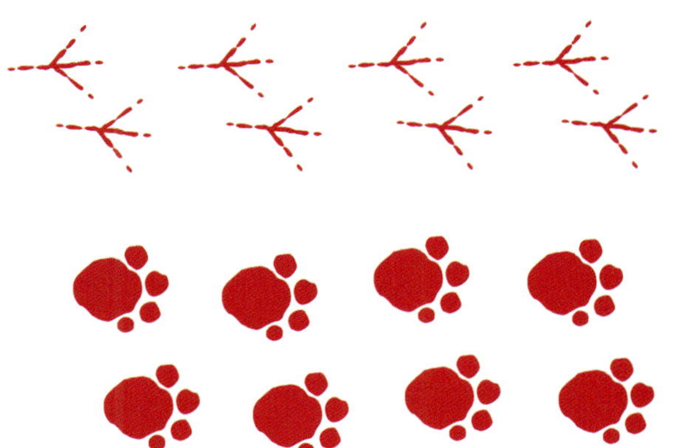

Ordering Information

Please call for current pricing

- Telephone: 360-730-2360 (in Washington)
- Toll-free: 1-888-568-9806
- FAX: 360-730-2355
- E:mail - dave@simonandbarklee.com

Books are available individually or in packages for educators.

Discounts apply for package purchases.

Packages can be customized to order.

Watch for future Simon and Barklee books

2001

France, England and Germany

2002

Africa, Mexico, Peru

2003

China, Japan,
Australia and New Zealand

2004

Russia, India, Turkey

AND BEYOND......

More to come

Author Available for School Visits and Speaking Engagements

Would you like for Simon and Barklee's author to visit your school or speak to your group? Please let us know. He would be happy to visit individual classes, an assembly, or to speak to an educators group or meeting. Telephone the toll-free number listed on the previous page to schedule a visit.

A division of Simon & Barklee, Inc.